SCIENCE 608
Spaceship Earth

LIFEPAC Test is located in the center of the booklet. Please remove before starting the unit.

Author:
Barry G. Burrus, M.Div., M.A., B.S.

Editors:
Alpha Omega Staff

Illustrations:
Alpha Omega Staff

Revision Editor:
Alan Christopherson, M.S.

MEDIA CREDITS:
Pages 6: © Znovenko, iStock, Thinkstock; **15:** © Joachim Angeltun , iStock, Thinkstock; **18:** © pixelparticle, iStock, Thinkstock; **20:** © Stocktrek Images, iStock, Thinkstock; © alex-mit, iStock, Thinkstock; **25:** © CarolMRobinson, iStock, Thinkstock; **27:** © Photos.com, Thnkstock; **38:** © DavidSzabo, iStock, Thinkstock; **39:** © flowgraph, iStock, Thinkstock; **40:** © Joe Rainbow, iStock, Thinkstock; **43:** © ChrisGorgio, iStock, Thinkstock; **45:** © graphics.vp, iStock, Thinkstock; **46:** © mark higgins, iStock, Thinkstock.

Alpha Omega
PUBLICATIONS

804 N. 2nd Ave. E.
Rock Rapids, IA 51246-1759

Spaceship Earth

Introduction

In His wisdom and love, God created a beautiful home for us – the earth. Our home, the earth, can also be compared to a "spaceship." What is a spaceship? It is a vehicle carrying human beings and other cargo that travels through space. Our earth is like that. Earth is constantly in motion through the vast spaces of the universe. It rotates about its axis. It orbits around the sun. It travels with the rest of our solar system around the center of our **galaxy** – the Milky Way Galaxy. Finally, it travels with the rest of the Milky Way Galaxy through the Universe. Truly, the earth is a huge "spaceship," carrying us and all living things with it as it journeys through space.

In this LIFEPAC®, you will learn more about the earth's size, shape, and motion through space. You will also learn about the relationship of the earth to the moon and the sun, and how these three bodies interact to form eclipses. Finally, you will learn more about our solar system which includes the sun and its eight planets.

Objectives

Read these objectives. These objectives tell what you should be able to do when you have completed this LIFEPAC. When you have completed this LIFEPAC, you should be able to do the following:

1. Describe earth's size and shape and its motion through space.

2. Explain how night and day occur on the earth.

3. Define the time zones on earth and be able to locate the Prime Meridian and the International Date Line.

4. Explain the seasons of the year and how they occur.

5. Describe what happens when the vernal and autumnal equinoxes occur.

6. Describe what happens during a solar eclipse and a lunar eclipse.

7. Name and describe the main parts of our solar system.

8. List the eight major planets of our solar system from the sun outward and describe the relative size and composition of each planet.

9. Define and describe some major characteristics of asteroids, comets, and meteoroids.

Survey the LIFEPAC. Ask yourself some questions about this study and write your questions here.

1. EARTH'S MOTION

When you look at the earth around you each day, it appears to be very fixed and **stable**. Yet, we know that the earth is actually in motion in several ways. The fact that we have day and night shows that the earth rotates about its axis, with half of it **illuminated** by the sun and the other half dark because it is hidden from the sun. In addition, the fact that we have four seasons of the year is explained by the motion of the earth around the sun once a year. The earth also moves through space in other ways, and you will learn more about the various movements of "spaceship Earth" in this section of the LIFEPAC.

Even though the earth is constantly in motion, God has wonderfully designed our earth to support life. He did this by giving the earth a definite size and shape. He also designed the earth to support life by placing the earth in a position from the sun that allows the right life-supporting temperatures to exist on earth. He also placed adequate water, oxygen, and carbon dioxide upon earth to support life. God designed the motions of the earth to occur in regular cycles, such as day, night, and the four seasons of the year. This regular motion of the earth also helps to support and sustain life on earth.

Throughout history, human beings have used the regular motions of the earth to express the passage of time. They have also devised different ways of designating *position* and location on the earth. In this section of the LIFEPAC, you will also learn more about the way humans in most nations of the world today designate time and location upon earth.

Section Objectives

Review these objectives. When you have completed this section, you should be able to:

1. Describe Earth's size and shape and its motion through space.
2. Explain how night and day occur on the earth.
3. Define the time zones on earth and be able to locate the Prime Meridian and the International Date Line.
4. Explain the seasons of the year and how they occur.
5. Describe what happens when the vernal and autumnal equinoxes occur.

Vocabulary

Study these words to enhance your learning success in this section.

autumnal equinox (ô tum nəl ē kwə noks). Occurs on September 22 or 23, when the days and nights are equal.

ellipse (i lips). An egg-shaped figure similar to a circle which also describes the path or orbit of one body around another.

galaxy (gal ək sē). A system of numerous associated stars traveling together through the universe. Our galaxy is the Milky Way Galaxy, containing hundreds of billions of stars.

illuminated (i lü mə nāt ed). Supplied or brightened with light.

longitude (lon jə tüd). A distance measured in degrees east or west on the earth's surface from the Prime Meridian.

meridian (mə rid ē ən). An imaginary line running north-south around the earth through the North and South Poles.

orbit (ôr bit). Curving path that a moving body takes around another body in space.

rotation (rō tā shən). The action or process of rotating or turning about an axis or center.

sidereal day (sī dir ē əl dā). The time that the earth takes to make exactly one complete rotation to the very same position on earth compared to far distant stars; it is 23 hours 56 minutes 4.091 seconds.

solar day (sō lər dā). The time that the earth takes to make one complete rotation relative to the sun; it is 24 hours.

stable (stā bəl). Firmly established; not changing, moving, or fluctuating.

vernal equinox (vėr nəl ē kwə noks). The spring equinox on March 19, 20, or 21 when the days and nights are of equal length.

Note: *All vocabulary words in this LIFEPAC appear in* **boldface** *print the first time they are used. If you are not sure of the meaning when you are reading, study the definitions given.*

Pronunciation Key: hat, āge, cãre, fär; let, ēqual, tėrm; it, īce; hot, ōpen, ôrder; oil; out; cup, pu̇t, rüle; child; long; thin; /ᵺH/ for then; /zh/ for measure; /u/ or /ə/ represents /a/ in about, /e/ in taken, /i/ in pencil, /o/ in lemon, and /u/ in circus.

| The size and shape of the Earth vary slightly in relation to one another.

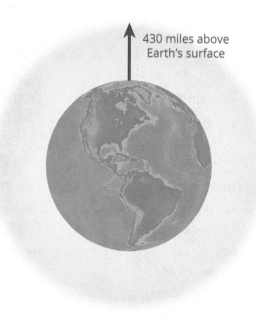

| Atmosphere above Earth

EARTH'S SIZE AND SHAPE

Before discussing the motion of "spaceship Earth," let us consider a few facts about "spaceship Earth" itself. Viewed from space, the earth appears as a large sphere (ball). It has vast swarms of white clouds, blue oceans, and brown and green land areas. At the top of the earth is the North Pole, and the South Pole is near the bottom of the earth. The areas surrounding the Poles are large, ice-covered areas that appear white. This view of the earth from space, showing its overall appearance, is truly beautiful. Let's consider some details about the overall size and shape of the earth.

Size and shape. The earth is shaped like a large sphere. However, the earth is not perfectly round. It is slightly flattened at the Poles. This means that the diameter of the earth measured from the North Pole to the South Pole is slightly less than the diameter across the middle of the earth at the equator. From Pole to Pole, the diameter of the earth is about 7,900 miles (12,714 kilometers). At the equator, the diameter of the earth is about 7,926 miles (12,756 kilometers). Therefore, the distance from Pole to Pole is 26 miles (42 kilometers) less than the diameter of the earth at the equator. This is why the earth is actually slightly flattened at the Poles, although it may look perfectly round when viewed from far away in space.

In the same way, the distance around the earth is shorter at the Poles than at the equator. At the Poles, the earth is 24,860 miles (40,008 kilometers) around. At the equator, it is slightly greater: 24,902 miles (40,075 kilometers) around. However, the equator is not actually the "fattest" part of the earth. The distance around the earth is greatest along a circle slightly south of the equator. Therefore, the earth's shape is a little bit like that of a pear, which has its fattest part just below its middle. But this bulge in the earth's shape is so small that the earth still looks like a perfectly round sphere when viewed from space.

The earth not only has a great size in volume and distance, it also has a very, very large mass. The mass of the earth is:
13,190,000,000,000,000,000,000,000 pounds
or
5,983,000,000,000,000,000,000,000 kilograms!

The atmosphere. So far, we have only considered the solid earth and the waters upon the earth when considering its size and shape. But there is another part of "spaceship Earth" that travels with it as it travels around the sun and through the universe. This is the *atmosphere* above the earth. Air surrounds the entire earth in the atmosphere. It is like a thick, clear, spherical layer surrounding the globe of the earth. The atmosphere extends as far as 430 miles (692 kilometers) above the surface of the earth. The air in the atmosphere gets thinner and thinner the greater the distance from the surface of the earth. Above 300 miles, the atmosphere is so thin that satellites and spacecraft orbiting the earth encounter almost no resistance from the air molecules and atoms.

Complete the following activity.

1.1 In the space below, draw a circle representing "spaceship Earth."

Place a dot at the top of the circle representing the North Pole and a dot at the bottom of the circle representing the South Pole. Draw a line between the North Pole and the South Pole. Just above this line, write the number of miles between the North Pole and South Pole as a diameter of the earth. Also write that number here. a. _____

Draw a horizontal line at the middle of the circle representing the equator. Just above that line, write the number of miles across the earth at the equator as a diameter of the earth. Also write that number here. b. _____

What is the difference between the two numbers? c. _____

Is the earth perfectly round? d. _____

Answer true or false.

1.2 _____ Earth can be called a "spaceship" because it is like a vehicle carrying humans and other cargo through space.

1.3 _____ Earth's only motions are to rotate about its axis and to orbit around the sun.

1.4 _____ Earth appears to us to be very fixed and stable, but it is not.

1.5 _____ The regular motions of the earth help support and sustain life.

1.6 _____ Viewed from space, earth appears as a large sphere.

1.7 _____ The earth is perfectly round.

1.8 _____ At the Poles, the earth is about 790 miles in diameter.

1.9 _____ The atmosphere of the earth extends to about 430 miles beyond the surface.

EARTH'S ROTATION

The motion of the earth that is most obvious is the one that produces day and night. Of course, ancient peoples thought that the sun traveled around the earth from east to west, producing day and night. Today, we know that it is actually the **rotation** of the earth that causes day and night. The rotation of the earth is the first type of motion that "spaceship Earth" experiences.

The earth rotates about an imaginary axis that extends through the North and South Poles. Rather than being straight up and down, the axis of the earth is tilted at 23.5 degrees from the vertical. The earth spins around this axis. Looking down at the earth from the North Pole, the earth would be spinning in a counterclockwise direction. One half of the earth is always illuminated as it faces the sun. The other half of the earth is always dark with night as it is turned away from the sun. As the earth rotates in a counterclockwise direction, people who have been in night will begin to see the light of the sun coming from the east. As the earth continues to rotate, they will see the sun "come up" in the east. These people will then experience daylight as their side of the earth rotates in the light of the sun. Finally, as night approaches, they will see the sun "set" in the west, and the sun will finally disappear below the horizon as the earth rotates and their location on the earth is hidden from the sun.

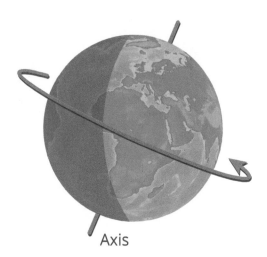

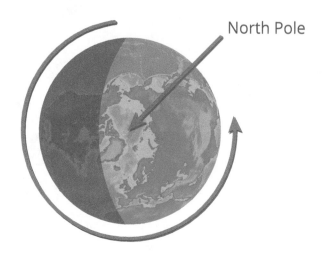

| The Earth is tilted on its axis, and rotates in a counterclockwise direction.

In relation to the sun, the earth takes 24 hours to make one complete rotation about its axis. This is called a **solar day**. In relation to the very same position on earth compared to far distant stars, however, the earth takes 23 hours 56 minutes 4.091 seconds to make one complete rotation. This is called a **sidereal day**. Why this difference? The answer has to do with the fact that the earth is also slowly orbiting around the sun as it rotates each day. Therefore, in relation to the sun, a point on the earth has to travel a small amount more each day for the same point on earth to be in a direct line with the sun. This accounts for the 3 minutes 55.909 seconds difference between a *solar day* and a *sidereal day*.

How fast do you travel as the earth rotates around its axis? The answer depends on your location on the surface of the earth. The speed due to rotation at the equator can be calculated by dividing the distance around the earth at the equator (the distance traveled in one rotation of the earth) by the time in a sidereal day. This would be 24,902 miles divided by 23 hours 56 minutes 4.091 seconds. The answer is 1,040.4 miles per hour. So, even if you were "standing still" at the equator, you would actually be traveling 1,040.4 miles per hour due to the rotation of the earth.

If you were located half way between the equator and the North Pole, your speed would be less than it would be at the equator because the distance around the earth at that point is less: about 17,607 miles. Therefore, dividing that distance by the time in a sidereal day would give you a speed of 735.7 miles per hour due to the rotation of the earth. Earth's motion due to rotation is much faster than it normally seems as you look around you each day!

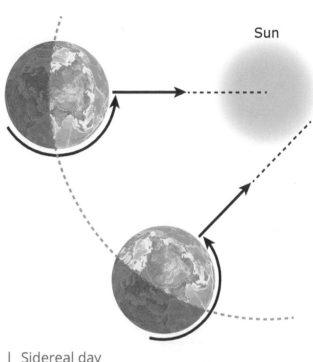

Sun

| Sidereal day

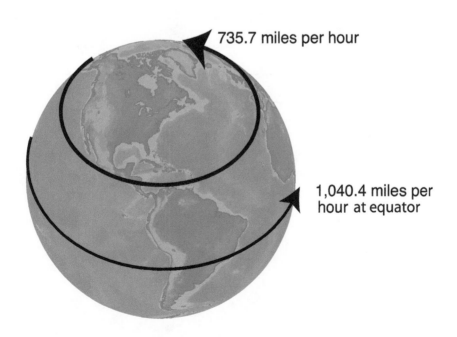

735.7 miles per hour

1,040.4 miles per hour at equator

| Speeds on the Earth due to rotation

Answer these questions.

1.10 Why do we have day and night on the earth?

_____

_____

1.11 What is the difference between a *solar day* and a *sidereal day* ?

_____

_____

_____

_____

_____

_____

1.12 Why does your speed of motion due to rotation of the earth depend on your location?

_____

_____

_____

_____

_____

_____

_____

TIME

From ancient times, people have observed that day and night alternate as the earth rotates about its axis. Therefore, the "day" became a convenient way to measure the passage of *time*. It also became convenient to divide the periods of day and night into smaller periods of time, such as the hour, minute, and second. People also had to agree on the *beginning* of each solar day (24 hours). The Babylonians began their day at sunrise. The ancient Jews began their day at sunset. The Egyptians and Romans began their day at midnight. Today, most places in the world have adopted the practice of beginning the new day at midnight.

Each "day" begins at midnight. A full day lasts 24 hours (*a solar day*). In most countries of the world, the day is divided into two parts of 12 hours each. The hours from midnight to noon are the A.M. (before noon). The hours from noon to midnight are the P.M. (after noon). Therefore, 8:00 A.M. would be 8 hours after midnight, and 8:00 P.M. would be 8 hours after noon. The military often denotes time on a 24-hour basis, such as 0000 for midnight and the start of a new day, 0800 for eight o'clock in the morning (8:00 A.M.), 1200 for noon, and 2000 for eight o'clock at night (8:00 P.M.).

As the earth rotates, where should people say the "day" begins for the whole earth? The solution to this problem has been solved by designating specific "lines" and "zones" about the earth.

| Ancient peoples measured time by day and night.

Longitude. To conveniently divide the globe of the earth into parts, imaginary lines are drawn from the North Pole to the South Pole. A circle surrounding the earth at the equator would consist of 360 "degrees" of angular measurement (written as 360°). Therefore, by dividing the entire globe into parts for each hour of a 24-hour day, we would divide 360° by 24 hours, or 15° for each hour of the day on earth. The imaginary lines from the North to the South Pole are then placed 15° apart. These imaginary lines are called meridians of longitude. By agreement among the nations of the world, the earth's surface is divided into 24 time zones separated by 15° of longitude. The division into these twenty-four time zones is called *Standard Time*.

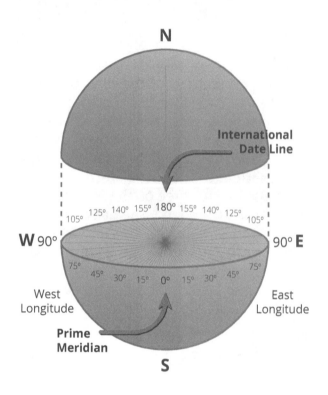

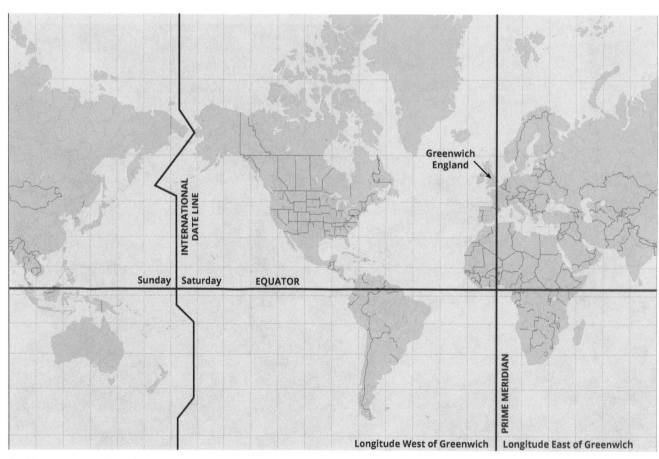

| The International Date Line

The *Prime Meridian* is designated as the 0° location on earth. It runs through Greenwich, England, which is a suburb in Southeast London. From that imaginary line, the time zones run east and west. These meridians run 180° east and 180° west. For example, the first time zone in the United States is located about 75° west of the Prime Meridian at Greenwich. The 180° meridian is on the other side of the earth exactly opposite the Prime Meridian at Greenwich. This 180° meridian is called the *International Date Line*. By international agreement among the countries of the earth, this 180° meridian – the International Date Line – is where the new calendar day begins.

The International Date Line does not follow the 180° meridian exactly. It zigzags through the Pacific Ocean to avoid dividing an island or land area into two different dates.

Time Zones. The continental United States has four time zones. They are the Eastern, Central, Mountain, and Pacific time zones. Like the International Date Line, these time zones in the United States do not follow specific lines of longitude exactly. They zigzag through the United States to avoid dividing cities into two different time zones. They are approximately located at 75°, 90°, 105°, and 120° west of the Prime Meridian.

There is one hour difference between adjoining time zones in the U.S. For example, when it is 7:00 P.M. in the Eastern time zone, it is 6:00 P.M. in the Central time zone. Notice that there is a three-hour difference between the Eastern time zone and the Western time zone. When it is 7:00 P.M. in New York City, New York, it is 4:00 P.M. in Los Angeles, California.

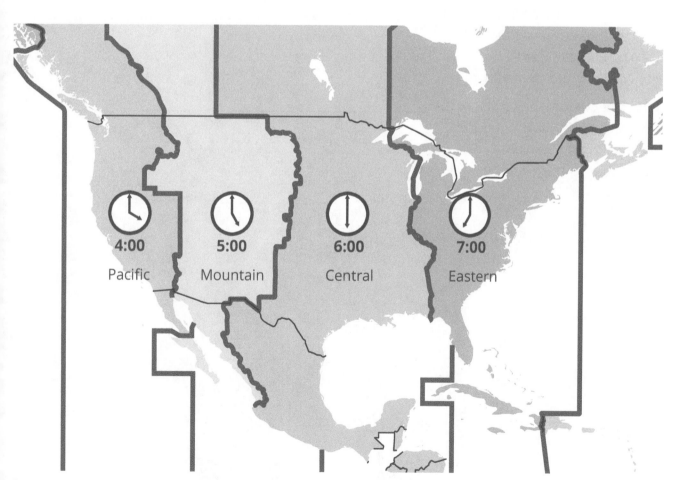

| Time Zones of the United States

Write the correct letter and answer on the line.

1.13 The ancient Jews began their day at _____ .

    a. sunset   b. sunrise   c. midnight   d. noon

1.14 Today, most places in the world have adopted the practice of beginning the new day at

    _____ .

    a. sunset   b. sunrise   c. midnight   d. noon

1.15 In the military services, 6:00 P.M. would be written as _____ .

    a. 6:00   b. 0600   c. 1200   d. 1800

1.16 A circle surrounding the earth at the equator would consist of _____ "degrees" of angular measurement.

    a. 15   b. 90   c. 180   d. 360

1.17 The division of the earth's surface into twenty-four time zones is called

    _____ .

    a. Greenwich time   b. Standard time   c. Meridian time   d. Clock time

1.18 The 0° meridian is known as the _____ .

    a. International Date Line

    b. Prime Meridian

    c. Longitude Time Zone

1.19 The calendar day starts at the _____ .

    a. International Date Line

    b. Prime Meridian

    c. Eastern Time Zone

1.20 In the continental United States, there are _____ time zones.

    a. three   b. four   c. five

EARTH'S ORBIT

The second major motion of the "spaceship Earth" is its **orbit**, or revolution, around the sun. To make one complete revolution around the sun, the earth takes 365 days, 6 hours, 9 minutes, and 4.091 seconds! We normally define a year as 365 days. Therefore, since it actually takes the earth a little more than 365 days to orbit about the sun, we add an extra day to the year every four years on February 29. This is called a *leap year*. A leap year has 366 days.

During its orbit around the sun in a year, the earth travels 595 million miles (958 million kilometers). During this journey, the earth travels at an average speed of 66,000 miles an hour (107,200 kilometers an hour)! Therefore, not only are you in motion due to the rotation of the earth, you are also traveling very fast on "spaceship Earth" as it speeds around the sun!

An *orbit* is the curving path that a moving body takes around another body in space. Although the earth's orbit around the sun might appear circular on some drawings, it is not. It is actually somewhat elliptical. This orbital path is known as an **ellipse**. All the other planets in our solar system travel in an ellipse around the sun, too. (You will learn more about our solar system in Section III of this LIFEPAC.) Even spacecraft and satellites that circle the earth have orbits that are ellipses.

During the earth's journey around the sun, its distance from the sun varies from 94,500,000 miles in the summer to 91,500,000 miles in the Northern Hemisphere's winter. Therefore, you can see that the orbital path is not a perfect circle, since the distance would always remain the same if it were a circle. The *average* distance of the earth from the sun in its yearly elliptical orbit is 93,000,000 miles.

Newton's Laws. In a previous LIFEPAC, you learned about Sir Isaac Newton's Laws of Motion. Two of these laws help to explain

| The Earth's orbit around the Sun

earth's orbit. They are (1) *the Law of Inertia*, and (2) *the Universal Law of Gravitation*. The *Law of Inertia* states that an object at rest tends to stay at rest, and an object in motion tends to stay in motion in a straight line, unless acted upon by an outside, unbalanced force. The *Universal Law of Gravitation* states that all objects (masses) in the universe pull or attract one another. The larger the object, the greater the pull.

"Spaceship Earth" continues to move around the sun because of inertia. It does not travel in a straight line because of the pull of the sun's gravity. The pull of gravity is an unbalanced force that holds the earth and the other planets in our solar system in orbit around the sun.

Newton's Laws do not explain everything about the orbit of the earth around the sun. For example, who set the earth orbiting around the sun in the first place? These and many other things about our earth, solar system, and universe cannot be satisfactorily or fully explained by scientific laws and theories. By faith, we know that God is the creator and sustainer of the entire universe. It was God who set the planets, including the earth, in orbit about the sun. God has created an orderly universe, and humans can discover laws that God has established that help explain certain things about His creation. But, by faith, we know that God and

Jesus Christ hold ultimate power in the whole universe, and it is by that power that all things continue to exist. As Scripture says: Who is the image of the invisible God, the firstborn of every creature: For by him were all things created, that are in heaven, and that are in earth, visible and invisible, whether they be thrones, or dominions, or principalities, or powers: all things were created by him, and for him: And he is before all things, and by him all things consist (Colossians 1:15-17).

Seasons. The orbit of earth around the sun *and* the earth's tilt on its axis cause the seasons of the year: fall, winter, spring, and summer. Since the earth is tilted at an angle of 23.5°, the Northern Hemisphere is tilted more toward the sun and receives more light energy during the months of the summer. Therefore, the temperatures are higher and the daylight hours are longer. This is true even though the earth in its orbit is actually farther away from the sun in the summer than in the winter. The tilt of the earth in the summer allows the sun's rays to more directly fall on the Northern Hemisphere, and this has more effect on the earth's temperature than its distance from the sun. In the winter, the opposite is true: the Northern Hemisphere is tilted away from the sun; therefore, it receives less solar energy, even though the earth is actually closer to the sun in winter than in summer. Thus, in the winter months, temperatures are colder and the daylight hours are shorter in the Northern Hemisphere. Note that the seasons are reversed in the Southern Hemisphere.

It is also important to note that the North Pole area will be totally illuminated by the sun in summer during an entire rotation of the earth during 24 hours, while the South Pole will be totally in darkness during this time. In summer months for the Northern Hemisphere, the northernmost regions of the earth experience daylight for the entire 24 hours and the sun never fully sets. In the winter, it remains dark during the entire 24 hours, and the sun never fully rises!

Equinoxes. In the spring and fall, the position of the earth's orbit around the sun and the tilt of the earth allow the day and night to be an *equal* amount of time. This happens on March 19, 20, or 21 to start the spring season and is known as the **vernal equinox**. The word *vernal* means *spring*. The word *equinox* means "equal night," referring to the fact that the nighttime and the daylight are equal lengths on that day. Also on that day, the sun is directly overhead at noon on the equator. Following that day, the daylight hours become longer in the Northern Hemisphere. In the fall, on September 22 or 23, the daylight and nighttime become equal again on the **autumnal equinox**. Again on that day, the sun is directly overhead at noon on the equator. Following that day, the daylight hours become shorter in the Northern Hemisphere.

Match these items.

1.21 _____ orbit

1.22 _____ leap year

1.23 _____ one orbit of earth

1.24 _____ ellipse

1.25 _____ earth from sun

1.26 _____ inertia

1.27 _____ Sir Isaac Newton

1.28 _____ tilt of earth

1.29 _____ International Date Line

1.30 _____ summer

a. shape of earth's orbital path around sun

b. helps earth continue to go around sun

c. 23.5°

d. daylight lasts 24 hours at North Pole

e. gravity

f. curving path that a moving body takes around another body in space

g. 595 million miles

h. 366 days

i. 0° meridian

j. 93 million miles

k. laws of inertia and gravitation

l. 180° meridian

Answer the following questions.

1.31 How are the vernal and autumnal equinoxes the same?

_____

_____

_____

1.32 How are the vernal and autumnal equinoxes different?

_____

_____

_____

1.33 Can scientific laws and theories explain everything about our universe? _____

Explain your answer. _____

_____

_____

_____

EARTH'S OTHER MOTIONS

You have learned that "spaceship Earth" has motion as it rotates daily and as it orbits around the sun yearly. But "spaceship Earth" also has motion in two additional ways. First, it moves with our solar system around the center of our galaxy – the Milky Way Galaxy. Second, it moves with our entire galaxy as it expands outward from what is thought to be the center of the universe. Let's briefly explore each of these additional motions of "spaceship Earth."

Motion in the Milky Way Galaxy. Earth, our sun, and the other planets in our solar system, are all located in a huge *galaxy* called the Milky Way Galaxy. This galaxy consists of hundreds of billions of stars, one of which is our own sun. The Milky Way Galaxy is a *spiral galaxy*, and has a spiral shape (like a gigantic pinwheel). All of the stars in the various spirals, including our sun and solar system, rotate about the center of the galaxy. Scientists estimate that our sun takes about 250 million years to rotate once around the center of our galaxy! Based upon the approximate location of our sun with the galaxy, the sun – and "spaceship Earth" along with it – would be traveling at a speed of about 101,000 miles per hour as it rotates about the center of the Milky Way Galaxy!

| The Milky Way is a spiral galaxy.

Motion with the Galaxy in the Universe. The final motion of "spaceship Earth" that we will consider is on such a large scale that it is almost impossible to imagine it! Our galaxy, along with billions of other galaxies throughout the known universe, is thought by many scientists to be expanding outward, away from other galaxies. If this is so, then our tiny "spaceship Earth" (compared with the size of the galaxies) is also in motion due to this outward expansion of galaxies in the universe. God has created an incredibly large universe; however He is greater than all the universe! What an awesome God we serve here on "spaceship Earth"!

| Side view of the Milky Way Galaxy

*"From the rising of the sun unto the going down of the same
the LORD'S name is to be praised." Psalm 113:3*

Please study and memorize this verse. It will be on the LIFEPAC Test.

 Search the Internet or library.

1.34 Using the Internet, library, or other resources, find out more about our Milky Way Galaxy and the galaxies nearby in our "Local Group" of galaxies. Write a half-page report on what you find, including information about the size, type, and number of stars in these galaxies.

TEACHER CHECK _____ _____
                                         initials   date

Review the material in this section in preparation for the Self Test. The Self Test will check your mastery of this particular section. The items missed on this Self Test will indicate specific areas where restudy is needed for mastery.

SELF TEST 1

Match these items (each answer, 3 points).

1.01	_____ orbit		a.	diameter of earth at Poles
1.02	_____ ellipse		b.	distance around earth at Poles
1.03	_____ inertia		c.	extent of earth's atmosphere
1.04	_____ 7,900 miles		d.	one orbit of earth around sun
1.05	_____ 24,860 miles		e.	distance from earth to sun
1.06	_____ 430 miles		f.	solar day
1.07	_____ 595 million miles		g.	sidereal day
1.08	_____ vernal		h.	spiral galaxy
1.09	_____ Milky Way		i.	of spring
1.010	_____ 24 hours		j.	helps earth continue to go around sun
			k.	shape of the earth's orbital path around sun
			l.	curving path that a moving body takes around another body in space

Answer true or false (each answer, 2 points).

1.011 _____ Earth can be called "spaceship" because it is like a vehicle carrying humans and cargo through space.

1.012 _____ The regular motions of the earth help support and sustain life.

1.013 _____ Viewed from space, the earth appears as a large sphere.

1.014 _____ The earth is perfectly round.

1.015 _____ Longitude is the distance measured in degrees east or west from the International Date Line.

1.016 _____ At any time, half the earth faces the sun and the other half faces away from the sun.

1.017 _____ Due to the earth's rotation, a person would be traveling faster at the equator than he would at a position halfway from the equator to the North Pole.

1.018 _____ The military denotes 1:00 P.M. as 1300.

1.019 _____ There are three time zones in the continental United States.

1.020 _____ The earth's path around the sun is a perfect circle.

Write the correct letter and answer on each line (each answer, 3 points).

1.021 The earth is tilted on its axis at an angle of _____ .
a. 15°   b. 23.5°   c. 180°

1.022 The ancient Jews began their day at _____ .
a. sunset   b. midnight   c. sunrise

1.023 Each time zone around the world represents about _____ of longitude.
a. 15°   b. 23.5°   c. 90°

1.024 The Prime Meridian runs through _____ .
a. Los Angeles, California   b. The Pacific Ocean   c. Greenwich, England

1.025 When it is 8:00 A.M. in New York, it is _____ in California.
a. 7:00 A.M.   b. 6:00 A.M.   c. 5:00 A.M.

1.026 A leap year has _____ days.
a. 365   b. 365.5   c. 366

1.027 The earth is closer to the sun during the Northern Hemisphere's _____ .
a. summer   b. fall   c. winter

1.028 The earth travels around the sun in an orbit shaped like a(n) _____ .
a. ellipse or oval   b. straight line   c. perfect circle

1.029 The seasons in the Southern Hemisphere are _____ from the ones in the Northern Hemisphere.
a. the same as   b. one season behind   c. reversed

1.030 The North Pole is dark 24 hours a day in _____ .
a. the summer   b. August   c. the winter

1.031 "Spaceship Earth" travels about _____ miles per hour in its journey around the center of the Milky Way Galaxy.
a. 150   b. 7,900   c. 101,000

Complete this list (each item, 2 points).

1.032 List four ways that "spaceship Earth" is in motion.

a. _____

b. _____

c. _____

d. _____

Answer these questions (each answer, 3 points).

1.033 How do night and day occur on the earth?

_____

_____

_____

1.034 What are the seasons of the year and how do they occur?

_____

_____

_____

_____

_____

_____

_____

1.035 What happens when the vernal and autumnal equinoxes occur?

_____

_____

_____

_____

_____

_____

_____

80 / 100   SCORE _____   TEACHER _____ _____
                                              initials   date

2. ECLIPSES

An **eclipse** is a total or partial obscuring (or darkening) of one celestial body by another. In this section of the LIFEPAC, we will be studying two types of eclipses: *solar* and *lunar*. Modern astronomers have learned much by studying eclipses. For instance, by observing solar eclipses, they have been able to determine the exact relative positions of the earth, sun, and moon. Observing eclipses has also helped astronomers to study possible changes in the strength of gravity and the size of the sun. The size of distant stars has been determined through the study of eclipses of other heavenly bodies.

Astronomers are able to predict eclipses with great accuracy. Although the earth and moon always cast shadows into space, eclipses do not occur every month. Because the moon's orbit is tilted about five degrees to the earth's orbit around the sun, the moon's shadow usually misses the earth, and so a solar eclipse only rarely occurs. Likewise, the moon is not usually eclipsed because it passes above or below the shadow of the earth. Thus, a solar or a lunar eclipse can only occur when the earth, sun, and moon are in nearly a straight line. Generally speaking, at least two solar eclipses and as many as three lunar eclipses may be seen each year from various places on the earth.

| A solar eclipse

Section Objective

Review this objective. When you have completed this section, you should be able to:

6. Describe what happens during a solar eclipse and a lunar eclipse.

Vocabulary

Study these words to enhance your learning success in this section.

eclipse (i klips). Complete or partial blocking of light passing from one body in space to another causing a shadow or darkness to fall on one of the bodies.

penumbra (pi num brə). The lightest part of the shadow (around the edges) outside of the complete shadow formed during an eclipse.

umbra (um brə). The darkest part of the shadow formed during an eclipse.

Pronunciation Key: hat, āge, cãre, fär; let, ēqual, tėrm; it, īce; hot, ōpen, ôrder; oil; out; cup, pút, rüle; child; long; thin; /ŦH/ for then; /zh/ for measure; /u/ or /ə/ represents /a/ in about, /e/ in taken, /i/ in pencil, /o/ in lemon, and /u/ in circus.

SOLAR ECLIPSES

A solar eclipse occurs when the sun, earth, and moon are in nearly a straight line. The moon's shadow sweeps across the face of the earth from west to east at a speed of about 2,000 miles per hour. Because the moon is in the middle between the earth and the sun, people in the eclipse zone will see the moon pass in front of the sun. How does this all happen?

The earth and moon always cast shadows into space. We are usually unaware of these shadows until an eclipse occurs. An eclipse takes place when a shadow is cast, resulting in a darkening effect. You may have noticed that some shadows are lighter on the edges than they are in the center. A shadow falls from the side of an object opposite the light source. If that light source is *smaller* than the object, such as a pinpoint of light, the shadow will be evenly dark (**umbra** only). However, if the light source is *larger* than the object, a shadow will be created with a *dark center*, the umbra, surrounded by a *lighter region*, the **penumbra**. The umbra is dark because the opaque object blocks all the light directed toward that part of the surface. (An opaque object is one through which no light can pass.) The penumbra appears when some of the light gets past the object and reaches the surface.

You can see an umbra and a penumbra in the shadow of your hand. Try this demonstration. Hold your hand a few feet from a lamp in a room with no other light. Place a piece of white paper on the other side of your hand. Your hand will cast a shadow on the paper. In the center of the shadow of each finger is the dark umbra. Around each umbra is a brighter penumbra.

In the illustration of "Shadows," note that shadow A forms a clearly defined shadow (umbra only) because the light source is *smaller* than the object. In shadow B we see a dark center (umbra) surrounded by a lighter region (penumbra) because the light source is *larger* than the object.

During a solar eclipse, the sun is darkened as the moon passes between the sun and the earth. The moon casts a shadow on the earth. People in the path of the shadow may see one of three types of eclipses. A *partial solar eclipse* is seen by those people living in the path of the *penumbral shadow*. A *total solar eclipse* is seen

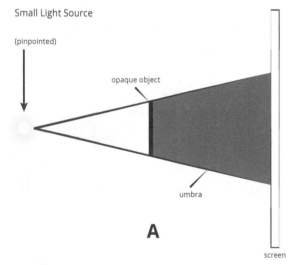

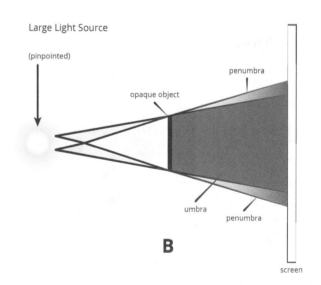

 Shadows

SCIENCE 608

LIFEPAC TEST

NAME _____

DATE _____

SCORE _____

SCIENCE 608: LIFEPAC TEST

Match these items (each answer, 2 points).

1. _____ orbit
2. _____ ellipse
3. _____ 7,900 miles
4. _____ 595 million miles
5. _____ eclipse
6. _____ umbra
7. _____ penumbra
8. _____ asteroids
9. _____ comets
10. _____ meteors
11. _____ meteorites

a. diameter of earth at Poles

b. one orbit of earth around sun

c. lighter outer region of a shadow

d. bright objects with a nucleus, coma, and tail

e. fall to earth

f. small rock or dust particles in outer space

g. distance from earth to sun

h. shooting stars

i. thousands of "small planets" orbiting the sun

j. curving path that a moving body takes around another body in space

k. shape of earth's orbital path around sun

l. dark center of a shadow

m. partial obscuring or darkening of one body by another

Answer true or false (each answer, 2 points).

12. _____ Earth can be called a "spaceship" because it takes up volume in space.

13. _____ The earth is perfectly round.

14. _____ Longitude is the distance measured in degrees from the Prime Meridian.

15. _____ There are four time zones in the continental United States.

16. _____ A fact is something that has been proven to be true.

17. _____ A total solar eclipse is seen by people living in the path of the umbral shadow.

18. _____ An annular solar eclipse occurs when the moon is at its farthest point from the earth during a total eclipse.

19. _____ Only sunspots can be called solar activity.

20. _____ Solar flares produce x-rays, radio waves, and clouds of atomic particles.

21. _____ All asteroids lie in the asteroid belt between Mars and Jupiter.

22. _____ Meteors are meteoroids that hit the earth.

Complete these lists (each answer, 2 points).

23.   List the eight major planets in order of their distance from the sun.

a. _____   b. _____

c. _____   d. _____

e. _____   f. _____

g. _____   h. _____

24.   List the four main motions of "spaceship Earth."

1. _____   2. _____

3. _____   4. _____

Write the correct letter and answer on each line (each answer, 2 points).

25.   The earth is tilted on its axis at an angle of _____ .
a. 15°   b. 23.5°   c. 180°

26   The ancient Jews began their day at _____ .
a. sunset   b. midnight   c. sunrise

27.   "Spaceship Earth" travels about _____ miles per hour in its journey around the center of the Milky Way Galaxy.
a. 150   b. 7,900   c. 101,000

28.   During a lunar eclipse, the moon appears to be darkened because _____ is casting a shadow on it.
a. the earth   b. the sun   c. Mars

29.   Since the moon is so small in size in relation to the earth, only a small area of planet earth will see a _____ .
a. lunar eclipse   b. corona   c. solar eclipse

30.   The sun contains _____ percent of the mass of the solar system.
a. 50   b. 80   c. 99

31.   In the sun, hydrogen is converted to _____ through nuclear fusion.
a. helium   b. carbon   c. water

32.   The sun rotates on it axis once every _____ .
a. 28 hours   b. 25 days 9 hours   c. 120 days

Write Psalm 113:3 from memory (this answer, 4 points).

33. _____

_____

_____

_____

_____

_____

_____

_____

Answer these questions (each answer, 5 points).

34. How do night and day occur on the earth?

_____

_____

_____

_____

_____

_____

_____

35. What are the seasons of the year and how do they occur?

_____

_____

_____

_____

_____

_____

_____

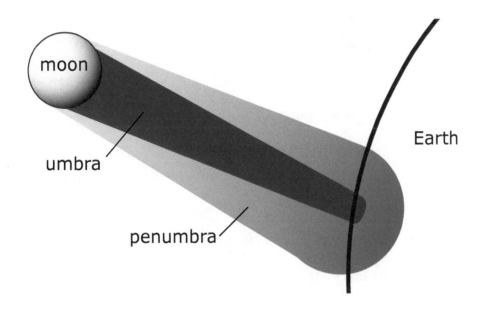

| The umbra and penumbra during a solar eclipse

by those people living in the path of the *umbral* shadow. An *annular solar eclipse* occurs when the moon is at its farthest point from the earth when a total eclipse occurs. In this case, the moon darkens only the middle of the sun, leaving a bright ring around the edges. In an annular eclipse, the light of the sun is not completely blocked.

Observing solar eclipses is fascinating, but should only be done in a safe manner. During a partial or annular eclipse, one should never look at the sun without proper eye protection. If using a telescope or any other optical instrument, make sure you use a filter to cover the front of the lens. One safe way to view these types of eclipses is to look at the sun's image as it is projected onto a piece of white paper. To do this, poke a small hole in an index card and hold a second card two or three feet behind it. The hole will project a small, inverted image of the sun's disk onto the lower card. The image will undergo all the phases of the real sun in the sky. To see the best possible image, make

| Missionaries projecting an eclipse on paper

sure that the hole is small, and hold the two cards about three feet apart. A total solar eclipse can only be safely viewed without protection when the disk of the sun is completely hidden and only the *corona* (the halo surrounding the sun) is visible. The corona is no brighter than a full moon.

Try the following experiment to learn more about eclipses.

Overview:

By going out into your backyard on a sunny day and using a simple coin, you will demonstrate the principle of a solar eclipse.

This supply is needed:

- a large coin, such as a quarter

Follow these directions. Place a check mark in the box as you complete each step.

☐ 1. Close one eye and look at a distant tree with your open eye.

☐ 2. Hold the coin at arms length in front of your eye.

☐ 3. Slowly move the coin closer to your open eye until it is directly in front of the eye.

Experiment 608.A Blackout

Answer these questions.

2.1 What happens to your view of the tree as the coin is brought closer and closer to your open eye?

_____

_____

_____

2.2 From this demonstration, as well as the previous text, we know that as the _____

passes between the _____ and the _____ , it blocks out light just like

the coin blocks your view of the tree.

2.3 In general, at least _____ solar eclipses and as many as _____ lunar

eclipses may be seen each year from various places on earth.

2.4 What are some things that astronomers have been able to learn by studying eclipses?

_____

_____

_____

_____

_____

_____

Answer true or false.

2.5 _____ A solar or lunar eclipse can only occur when the earth, sun, and moon are in nearly a straight line.

2.6 _____ A penumbral shadow is cast when the light source is smaller than the object.

2.7 _____ When the light source is larger than the object, a shadow is cast containing a dark center (umbra) surrounded by a lighter region (penumbra).

2.8 _____ A total solar eclipse is seen by people living in the path of the umbral shadow.

2.9 _____ An annular solar eclipse occurs when the moon is at its closest point from the earth during a total eclipse.

2.10 _____ A partial solar eclipse is seen by those people living in the path of the penumbral shadow.

2.11 _____ A corolla is the halo surrounding the sun which is seen during a total solar eclipse.

LUNAR ECLIPSES

A lunar eclipse takes place when the sun, earth, and moon are nearly in a straight line, with the earth being between the sun and the moon. The moon passes through the shadow of the earth.

There are three types of lunar eclipses. A *penumbral lunar eclipse* takes place when the moon enters only the penumbral shadow of the earth. A *partial lunar eclipse* occurs when the moon enters the umbral shadow of the earth without being entirely immersed in it. A *total lunar eclipse* occurs when the moon travels close to the earth's shadow and is entirely immersed within the umbral shadow.

The moon does not become completely dark during most lunar eclipses. In many cases, it appears reddish. This is because the earth's atmosphere bends part of the sun's light around the earth and toward the moon. The light appears red because the atmosphere scatters the other colors of the spectrum present in sunlight more than it does red. Recall from Science LIFEPAC 607 that red is the longest wavelength of light in the color spectrum. This also accounts for why the moon appears red. The red wavelength travels the farthest of all the colors in the spectrum.

One of the best ways to remember the difference between a solar eclipse and a lunar eclipse is to remember the meaning of the word eclipse. Eclipse, as previously defined, means the *darkening* of one celestial body by another body. During a lunar eclipse, the moon appears to be darkened because the earth is casting a shadow on it. When a solar eclipse occurs, the sun is darkened because the moon is casting a shadow as though it were blotting out the sun. Since the moon is so small in size in relation to the earth, only a small area of planet earth will see a solar eclipse.

Study the two diagrams which illustrate a solar and lunar eclipse. Carefully notice the position of the sun, moon, and the earth in both diagrams.

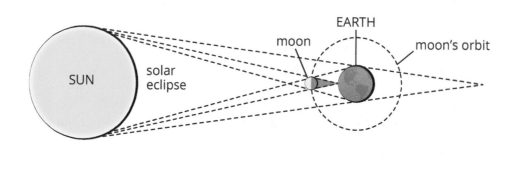

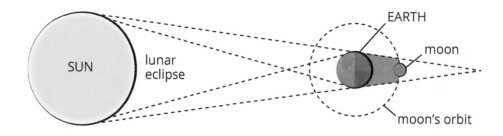

| Comparison of a solar eclipse (top) and a lunar eclipse (bottom)

Circle the letter of each correct answer.

2.12 A _____ takes place when the sun, earth, and moon are in nearly a straight line with the

earth being between the sun and the moon.

a. corona   b. lunar eclipse   c. solar eclipse

2.13 A penumbral lunar eclipse takes place when the moon enters only the _____ shadow of

the earth.

a. penumbral   b. umbral   c. outer

2.14 During a lunar eclipse, the moon appears to be darkened because _____ is casting a

shadow on it.

a. the sun   b. mars   c. the earth

2.15 A(n) _____ occurs when the moon enters the umbral shadow of the earth without being

entirely immersed in it.

a. total lunar eclipse   b. partial lunar eclipse   c. annular eclipse

2.16 Since the moon is so small in size in relation to the earth, only a small area of planet earth

will see a _____ .

a. lunar eclipse   b. corona   c. solar eclipse

2.17 The moon appears red during a lunar eclipse because red is the _____ wavelength of

light in the color spectrum present in sunlight.

a. longest   b. shortest   c. brightest

Try the following experiment to learn more about eclipses.

Overview:

A solar and lunar eclipse will be demonstrated using various sized balls and a bright light.

These supplies are needed:

- a large ball about the size of a basketball to represent the earth
- a small ball about the size of a tennis ball to represent the moon
- a strong light of about 100 watts or more
- a dark room

- NOTE: If your classroom is difficult to darken, you may use sunshine as your light source. In this case, you may want to use cardboard circles in place of balls. Cut one large circle about 8 inches in diameter to represent the earth. Cut one small circle about 3 inches in diameter to represent the moon.

Follow these directions. Place a check mark in the box as you complete each step.

☐ 1. Place a large ball (basketball) about 12 feet from the light source. Then place the small ball (tennis ball) in the shadow of the large ball. If you are using cardboard circles, hold the large cardboard up in the sunshine. Then, place the moon (small cardboard) in the earth's (large cardboard) shadow. When you have lined up the balls or cardboard in this manner, you have made a shadow fall on the moon. This shadow represents an eclipse of the moon.

☐ 2. Now, switch the balls or cardboard to make the shadow fall on the basketball or larger cardboard. Put the shadow of the smaller on the larger ball or cardboard circle. In effect, the sun is being darkened. If you were an observer on the earth, this condition would be a solar eclipse. When the moon comes between the sun and the earth, a solar eclipse occurs.

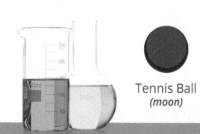

Tennis Ball *(moon)*	Basketball *(earth)*	Light Bulb *(sun)*

Experiment 608.B Eclipses

The preceding illustration shows how an eclipse can be artificially made. The moon (tennis ball) is darkened by a shadow. This shadow represents a lunar eclipse. You can reverse the position of the tennis ball and the basketball to represent a solar eclipse

Fill in each blank with the correct response.

2.18 A solar eclipse occurs when _____

_____

_____ .

2.19 *Eclipse* means: _____

2.20 A lunar eclipse occurs when _____

_____

_____ .

2.21 *Lunar* means: _____

2.22 *Solar* means: _____

2.23 Describe the difference between a solar and a lunar eclipse with respect to the positions of

the sun, moon, and earth. _____

_____

_____

_____

Read these paragraphs and complete the following activity.

In science, we often find theories and statements based on *opinion*. Frequently, these opinions have no scientific basis. An opinion is a view or idea about a matter. An opinion is based on individual judgment.

A *fact* is an actual event that has occurred. It is something that can be observed or known to have actual existence. For example, John says that cabbage tastes good. This statement is an opinion. Now, suppose that John says that cabbage is nutritious. This statement is a fact, because cabbage has been proven to have nutritional value.

Write *fact* or *opinion* before each statement.

2.24 a. _____ Mary believes that the world evolved.

b. _____ Planet earth is suspended in space.

c. _____ People have landed on the moon.

d. _____ Earth is a sphere.

e. _____ Studying astronomy is fun.

f. _____ Andrew said that the astronomy test was difficult.

g. _____ The sun may burn out at any time.

h. _____ Earth's rotation on its axis takes twenty-four hours.

i. _____ If given enough time, a star can evolve into a planet.

j. _____ The earth revolves around the sun in about 365 1/4 days.

k. _____ Earth is the only planet in our solar system that has been found to have enough water and oxygen for life.

l. _____ Spacecraft orbit the earth in an elliptically-shaped orbit.

Read this paragraph and complete the following activity.

Many of the words in science contain more than one or two syllables. Learning to divide words into syllables will help you learn how to spell them. Division into syllables is also necessary for proper pronunciation.

Use a dictionary to determine the proper way in which to divide the following words. This type of word division is known as syllabification.

2.25 a. syllabification _____

b. revolution _____

c. satellite _____

d. rotation _____

e. evolution _____

f. horizontally _____

g. vertically _____

h. elliptically _____

i. gravitation _____

j. inertia _____

↺ **Review the material in this section in preparation for the Self Test.** This Self Test will check your mastery of this particular section as well as your knowledge of the previous section.

SELF TEST 2

Match these items (each answer, 3 points).

2.01	_____ partial obscuring or darkening of one celestial body by another	a. opaque
2.02	_____ dark center of a shadow	b. red
2.03	_____ lighter outer region of a shadow	c. penumbral lunar eclipse
2.04	_____ object through which no light can pass	d. eclipse
2.05	_____ halo surrounding the sun	e. penumbra
2.06	_____ when moon enters only the penumbral shadow of the earth	f. total lunar eclipse
2.07	_____ when moon is entirely immersed within the umbral shadow	g. corona
2.08	_____ longest wavelength of light in the color spectrum	h. umbra

Answer true or false (each answer, 3 points).

2.09 _____ The word lunar means sun.

2.010 _____ A fact is something which has been proven to be true.

2.011 _____ An eclipse occurs once every month.

2.012 _____ Spacecraft orbit the earth in a circular orbit.

2.013 _____ A penumbral shadow is cast when the light source is smaller than the object.

2.014 _____ A total solar eclipse is seen by people living in the path of the umbral shadow.

2.015 _____ An annular solar eclipse occurs when the moon is at its farthest point from the earth during a total eclipse.

2.016 _____ A penumbra is the halo surrounding the sun which is seen during a total solar eclipse.

Fill in the blanks (each numbered problem, 4 points).

2.017 _____ helps the earth continue to go around the sun.

2.018 The average distance from the earth to the sun is _____ .

2.019 The four time zones of the United States are: a. _____ , b. _____ ,

c. _____ , and d. _____ .

2.020 Earth is tilted approximately _____ degrees.

2.021 Every fourth year is called a _____ .

2.022 A solar eclipse occurs when _____

_____

_____ .

2.023 A lunar eclipse occurs when _____

_____

_____ .

2.024 The pathway of a body in space is called its _____ .

Circle the letter of each correct answer (each answer, 2 points).

2.025 During a lunar eclipse, the moon appears to be darkened because _____ is casting a shadow on it.

a. the earth   b. the sun   c. Mars

2.026 Since the moon is so small in size in relation to the earth, only a small area of planet earth

will see a _____ .

a. lunar eclipse   b. corona   c. solar eclipse

2.027 During _____ there are 24 hours of daylight at the North Pole.

a. winter   b. spring   c. summer

2.028 One orbit of the earth around the sun equals _____ miles.

a. 5,280   b. 595 million   c. 360 million

2.029 _____ means "of spring."

a. solar   b. vernacular   c. vernal

Write a short answer to each of the following (each answer, 5 points).

2.030   Describe the difference between a solar and a lunar eclipse with respect to the positions of the sun, moon, and earth.

_____

_____

_____

_____

_____

_____

2.031   Why can't a solar eclipse be seen on every part of the earth?

_____

_____

_____

_____

_____

_____

80 / 100   **SCORE** _____   **TEACHER** _____ _____
                                                      initials   date

3. THE SOLAR SYSTEM

"Spaceship Earth" is located in the *solar system*. The solar system consists of the sun, the eight major planets orbiting around the sun, the moons of these planets, and **dwarf planets** like Pluto. In addition, **asteroids**, **comets**, and **meteoroids** are located within the solar system.

Finally, gas and dust are located in the space between all of these objects and are also part of our solar system. In this section of the LIFEPAC, you will learn more about the solar system and its various parts.

Section Objectives

Review these objectives. When you have completed this section, you should be able to:

7. Name and describe the main parts of our solar system.

8. List the eight major planets of our solar system from the sun outward and describe the relative size and composition of each planet.

9. Define and describe some major characteristics of asteroids, comets, and meteoroids.

Vocabulary

Study these words to enhance your learning success in this section.

asteroids (as tə roids). Small minor planets located in a belt between Mars and Jupiter.

comet (kom it). A bright body traveling through our solar system around the sun that is usually made up of particles of rock, metals, and frozen gases.

dwarf planet (dwôrf plan ət). A body that orbits the sun and has enough gravity to be nearly round in shape, but that has not cleared the neighborhood around its orbit of other objects like asteroids and is not a satellite of a planet.

meteor (mē tē ər). A mass of stony or stony-iron particles that enter the earth's atmosphere with enormous speed and is called a "shooting star." Most of them burn up in the earth's atmosphere.

meteorite (mē tē ə rī t). A meteor or meteor fragment that reaches the earth.

meteoroid (mē tē ə roid). Small piece of rock or dust that orbits the sun. When it enters earth's atmosphere, it is called a meteor.

solar flares (sō lər flãrz). A form of solar activity. They often occur near sunspots. When a solar flare occurs, huge amounts of energy are released in just a few minutes.

sunspots (sun spotz). A form of solar activity caused by magnetic fields. They appear dark blotches on the surface of the sun because they are areas where the temperature is about 1,500°F cooler than the normal surface temperature.

Pronunciation Key: hat, āge, cãre, fär; let, ēqual, tėrm; it, īce; hot, ōpen, ôrder; oil; out; cup, pùt, rüle; child; long; thin; /ŦH/ for then; /zh/ for measure; /u/ or /ə/ represents /a/ in about, /e/ in taken, /i/ in pencil, /o/ in lemon, and /u/ in circus.

THE SUN

Our sun is at the center of the solar system. It is actually a star, similar to the hundreds of billions of stars located in the Milky Way Galaxy. It is a medium-sized star. Compared with the rest of the objects in our solar system, however, the sun is huge. It has a diameter of 865,000 miles (1,392,000 kilometers)! Its mass is about 2,000,000,000,000,000,000,000 tons! That is 99 percent of the mass of our entire solar system!

The sun is composed mainly of two gases: hydrogen (about 92 percent) and helium (about 8 percent). The hydrogen in the sun is being converted into helium by a process called *nuclear fusion*. During this process, tremendous amounts of energy are produced. In fact, the sun is the primary source of all the energy in our solar system and on earth.

The temperature of the sun is extremely hot! Near the center, it is around 28,000,000°F. At the surface, it is around 10,000°F. The sun appears yellow because of the temperature of its outer surface.

Many kinds of activity happen on the surface of the sun. Together, all of these are called *solar activity*. Solar activity increases and decreases over a period of about 11 years. The primary forms of solar activity are **sunspots** and **solar flares**.

Sunspots. *Sunspots* are one form of solar activity. They appear as dark blotches on the surface of the sun. They appear darker than the rest of

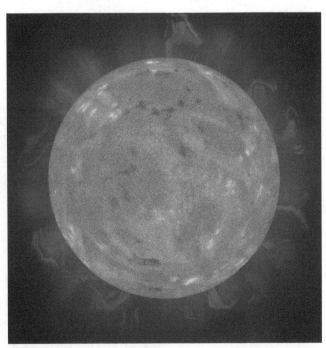

| Sunspots and solar flares

the surface because they are areas where the temperature is about 1,500°F cooler than the normal surface temperature. This cooler temperature is caused by a strong magnetic field in the sunspot area.

Sunspots can last several months, but most of them disappear in 10 days or less. As the sun rotates on its axis once every 25 days 9 hours, the sunspots appear to gradually move across the surface of the sun. Sunspots normally occur in groups. Individual sunspots can measure thousands of miles across.

Solar flares. *Solar flares* are a second form of solar activity. They often occur near sunspots. When a solar flare occurs, a huge amount of energy is released in just a few minutes. The temperature at these flare locations can rise to more than 2,000,000°F. Sometimes, with these flares, there are spectacular eruptions of hot gases, called *prominences*, that shoot out into space from the sun's surface at speeds of hundreds of miles per second.

Solar flares produce x-rays, radio waves, and clouds of atomic particles that shoot out into space. When these atomic particles from the sun's solar flare activity enter the earth's atmosphere, they cause bright lights in the sky called the *northern* and *southern lights*. These colorful lights can sometimes be seen in the night sky, usually in the polar regions of the earth. These atomic particles from solar flares can also upset the earth's magnetic fields and affect long-distance radio communications. The earth's atmosphere protects us from the harmful effects of solar x-rays, but astronauts in space must be protected from the harmful effects of these particles from solar flares.

| *Aurora borealis*; the northern lights.

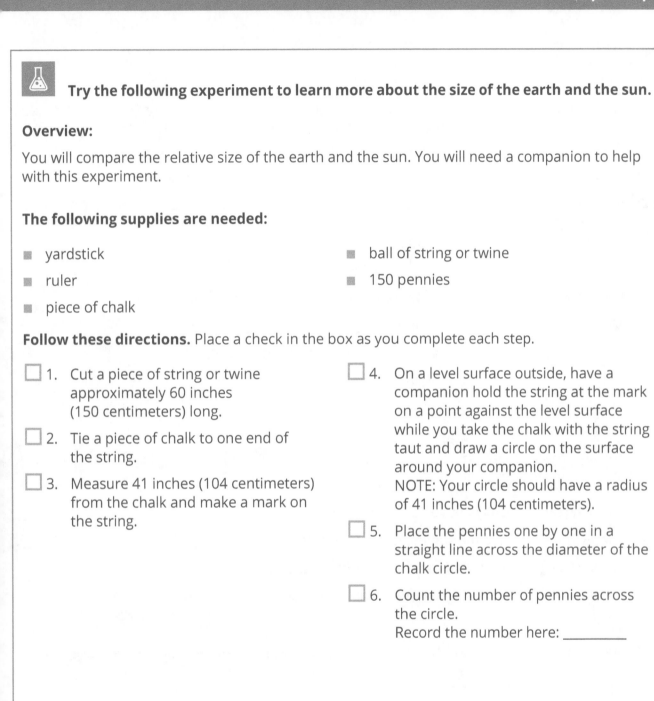

Try the following experiment to learn more about the size of the earth and the sun.

Overview:

You will compare the relative size of the earth and the sun. You will need a companion to help with this experiment.

The following supplies are needed:

- yardstick
- ruler
- piece of chalk
- ball of string or twine
- 150 pennies

Follow these directions. Place a check in the box as you complete each step.

☐ 1. Cut a piece of string or twine approximately 60 inches (150 centimeters) long.

☐ 2. Tie a piece of chalk to one end of the string.

☐ 3. Measure 41 inches (104 centimeters) from the chalk and make a mark on the string.

☐ 4. On a level surface outside, have a companion hold the string at the mark on a point against the level surface while you take the chalk with the string taut and draw a circle on the surface around your companion.
NOTE: Your circle should have a radius of 41 inches (104 centimeters).

☐ 5. Place the pennies one by one in a straight line across the diameter of the chalk circle.

☐ 6. Count the number of pennies across the circle.
Record the number here: _____

Experiment 608.C Compare the Size of the Earth and the Sun

Answer each of the following questions.

3.1 The penny represents the size of the earth and the chalk circle represents the size of the sun. How many times greater is the diameter of the sun than the earth? (Hint: How many pennies did it take to go across the circle?)

Answer: The diameter of the sun is _____ times greater than the earth.

3.2 If the diameter of the earth at the equator is 7,926 miles, then what is the diameter of the sun according to your experiment? (Hint: Use your answer in 3.1 and the diameter of the earth to calculate the diameter of the sun.)

Answer: _____ miles.

3.3 How does your answer in 3.2 compare with the number given in this section?

My answer from this experiment is a. _____ miles.

Diameter of sun from information in this section of the LIFEPAC:

b. _____ miles.

Fill in the correct answers.

3.4 The sun is a medium-sized _____ .

3.5 The sun contains about _____ percent of the mass of the solar system.

3.6 The sun consist mainly of two gases: a. _____ and b. _____ .

3.7 Energy is produced in the sun through the process of _____ .

3.8 The surface temperature of the sun is normally about _____ °F.

3.9 The various kinds of activity on the surface of the sun are called

_____ .

3.10 Sunspots appear on the sun's surface because the surface temperature in these areas is

_____ .

3.11 Spectacular eruptions of hot gases from the sun's surface are called

_____ .

3.12 _____ on the sun produce x-rays, radio waves, and clouds of atomic particles.

3.13 Atomic particles from the sun in the earth's atmosphere can produce the _____

_____ .

| The planets and dwarf planet Pluto

THE PLANETS AND THEIR MOONS

Outside the sun, the eight largest objects in the solar system are *planets*. Planets are objects that orbit the sun and are not moons (or satellites) of another object. All of the planets rotate on an axis and also orbit the sun. Going out from the sun, the names and order of the planets are as follows: Mercury, Venus, Earth, Mars, Jupiter, Saturn, Uranus, and Neptune.

Six of the eight planets also have moons (or satellites) in orbit around them. Mercury and Venus do not have moons, but all the rest do. For example, Earth has one moon ("The Moon"), Mars has two. The other four have between fourteen and sixty-seven moons. Astronomers continue to classify and reclassify moons and other planetary bodies. Imagine what the nighttime sky looks like from the surface of one of these other four planets.

The four planets nearest the sun (Mercury, Venus, Earth, and Mars) are called *terrestrial* (earth-like) planets. These terrestrial planets appear to consist mainly of rock and iron. They are among the smallest planets in the solar system.

The four largest planets (Jupiter, Saturn, Uranus, and Neptune) are called *giant* planets. They are also called *Jovian* planets (after Jupiter, since they all have similar larger sizes and composition.) These *giant* planets consist mainly of gases like helium, hydrogen, ammonia, and methane. All of these giant planets also have "rings" around them. Saturn's rings are particularly large and visible from earth with the aid of a telescope or binoculars.

Dwarf planets. Pluto was once known as the smallest, coldest, and most distant planet from the sun. On August 24, 2006, the International Astronomical Union formally downgraded Pluto from an official planet to a dwarf planet. A dwarf planet is a body that orbits the sun and has enough gravity to be nearly round in shape, but that has not cleared the neighborhood around its orbit of other objects like asteroids and is not a satellite of a planet. Other dwarf planets have been identified and more are expected to be discovered as more information is gathered.

Our knowledge of the planets increased dramatically with the space programs of the United States and Russia in the last 35 years of the 20th Century. During that time, space probes journeyed to the planets, taking many photographs and collecting a vast amount of scientific data. Recently, another dwarf planet was seen by the Hubble telescope. Today, much information about the planets is available on the Internet and in libraries. In the following activities, you will be asked to research some of this information to learn more about the planets of our solar system.

Answer true or false.

3.14 _____ Planets are objects that orbit the sun and are not moons (or satellites) of another object.

3.15 _____ Pluto is one of the eight major planets in the solar system.

3.16 _____ Mercury and Venus do not have moons, but all the rest of the planets do.

3.17 _____ The four planets nearest the sun are called terrestrial (earth-like) planets.

3.18 _____ All of the giant planets have "rings" around them.

Search the Internet or library.

3.19 Do some research on the planets on the Internet, at the library, or use other resources in order to complete the following chart on the planets:

PLANETS FROM THE SUN OUTWARD	DIAMETER (MILES OR KM)	DISTANCE FROM THE SUN (MILES OR KM)	NUMBER OF MOONS	LENGTH OF DAY (HOURS)	LENGTH OF YEAR (YEARS OR DAYS)
Mercury					
Venus					
Earth					
Mars					
Jupiter					
Saturn					
Uranus					
Neptune					

Complete the following activity.

3.20 Choose one of the planets other than Earth that interests you, and write a half- to full-page report on it.

My choice is _____ .

Include information on the composition of the planet, its temperatures, and what its atmosphere and surface are like. Also include the names and information about any moons the planet has. Include information about spacecraft that have visited the planet. If possible, include a picture or drawing of the planet with your report.

TEACHER CHECK _____ _____
initials   date

ASTEROIDS, COMETS, AND METEOROIDS

You have learned about the sun and the eight planets in our solar system. Now you will learn about some of the other objects that make up our solar system.

Asteroids. In a "belt" located between the orbits of Mars and Jupiter, thousands of small rocks called *asteroids* (or small planets) are orbiting the sun. They lie in the "asteroid belt." Some asteroids do not lie in this belt, but orbit around the sun in long elliptical paths that bring them close to the earth and sun. Perhaps as many as 90,000 asteroids exist, with most of them located in the asteroid belt. The paths of many individual asteroids have been identified so far by astronomers. About 30 asteroids have diameters greater than 120 miles (190 kilometers). The largest of them, Ceres, now classified as a dwarf planet, has a diameter of 567 miles (913 kilometers). Many other asteroids are less than 1 mile across (1.6 kilometers).

Comets. A *comet* is a bright object in space with a nucleus made up of frozen water, carbon dioxide, methane and ammonia, with dust and rocky material buried in it. Comets orbit in long elliptical paths from the outer edges of our solar system around the sun. As a comet gets nearer the sun, the heat causes the ice to start melting. Gas and dust are given off, forming a large sphere around the nucleus. This sphere is called the *coma*. The dust and gas stream out into space, sometimes for a hundred million miles! This is the *tail* of the comet. Sometimes the earth passes through the remnants of comet tails, and *meteor showers* occur. The Perseids, remnants of comet Swift-Tuttle, are some of the brightest seen in the nighttime sky. The Perseids are visible on August 12 every year. Meteor showers from other comets that have passed through the solar system can be seen other nights of the year.

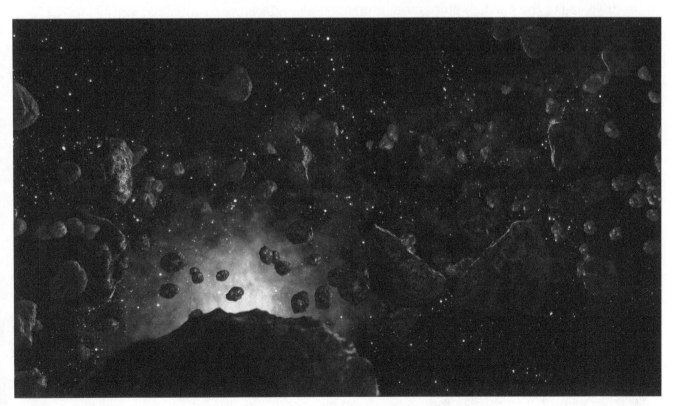

| An illustration of the asteroid belt

Comets are usually classified as *long-period* comets or *short-period* comets. Long-period comets take 200 years or more to orbit the sun. Short-period comets take less than 200 years to orbit the sun. One of the best-known short-period comets is Halley's comet, named after the English astronomer who first calculated and predicted its orbit, Edmond Halley. Halley's comet takes 76 years to complete an orbit. It was last visible in our part of the solar system in 1986. The next appearance of this space visitor will be in the year 2062.

Meteoroids. There are a great many particles of dust and very small rocks in our solar system called *meteoroids*. They can only be seen when they enter earth's atmosphere and burn up. When they enter the atmosphere, they are called *meteors*, or "shooting stars." Perhaps you have seen some of these race quickly across the night sky. Most meteors are about the size of a grain of sand and burn up quickly in the earth's atmosphere.

Sometimes, however, a meteor is larger and will actually fall to the earth. Meteors that aren't burned up in the atmosphere and are able to crash into the earth's surface are called *meteorites*. About 500 **meteorites** reach the earth each year, and most of these are about the size of a pebble. Almost all of them are unable to cause any kind of damage. However, on October 9, 1992, many people in the midwestern states of the U.S. saw a fireball that was as bright as a quarter moon light up the sky for about 15 seconds. A few moments later, a woman in Peekskill, New York was startled when she heard a loud crash. She went outside and found the rear end of her car smashed and a football-sized rock lying next to it. Authorities confirmed that the heavy rock, still warm, was indeed a meteorite. Larger meteorites have fallen to the earth, creating craters like those seen on the moon. These meteorite craters vary in size from less than a mile across, like "Meteor Crater" in northern Arizona. Meteor Crater measures about 3/4 mile across and 575 feet deep. Other craters found on earth measure up to 95 miles across. Therefore, "spaceship Earth" is sometimes visited by other travelers in our amazing solar system!

| Meteor Crater in northern Arizona was caused by a meteorite impact.

Complete this list.

3.21 List the eight planets of the solar system in order of their distances from the sun:

a. _____   b. _____   c. _____

d. _____   e. _____   f. _____

g. _____   h. _____

Match the following items.

3.22 _____ asteroids

3.23 _____ Ceres

3.24 _____ Halley

3.25 _____ comets

3.26 _____ meteoroids

3.27 _____ meteors

3.28 _____ meteorites

a. dust particles and small rocks that cannot be seen until they enter earth's atmosphere

b. fall to earth

c. the distance from the earth to the sun

d. solar flares

e. shooting stars

f. well-known comet

g. bright objects with nucleus, coma, and tail

h. thousands of "small planets" orbiting the sun

i. largest diameter asteroid, now classified as a dwarf planet

Before you take this last Self Test, you may want to do one or more of these self checks.

1. _____ Read the objectives. See if you can do them.
2. _____ Restudy the material related to any objectives that you cannot do.
3. _____ Use the **SQ3R** study procedure to review the material:
   a. **S**can the sections.
   b. **Q**uestion yourself.
   c. **R**ead to answer your questions.
   d. **R**ecite the answers to yourself.
   e. **R**eview areas you did not understand.
4. _____ Review all vocabulary, activities, and Self Tests, writing a correct answer for every wrong answer.

SELF TEST 3

Answer true or false (each answer, 2 points).

3.01 _____ The Sun is a large-sized star.

3.02 _____ All activity on the sun's surface is called solar activity.

3.03 _____ Sunspots rarely appear in groups.

3.04 _____ Solar flares produce x-rays, radio waves, and clouds of atomic particles.

3.05 _____ The planet Mercury does not have a moon.

3.06 _____ Some asteroids do not lie in the asteroid belt.

3.07 _____ The sun is composed primarily of hydrogen and oxygen.

3.08 _____ Comets orbit in short, circular paths around the sun.

3.09 _____ Halley's comet takes 5 years to complete an orbit.

3.010 _____ Meteors are meteoroids that hit the earth.

3.011 _____ Earth rotates west to east.

Match these items (each answer, 3 points).

3.012 _____ Jupiter

3.013 _____ Venus

3.014 _____ Jovian planets

3.015 _____ solar activity

3.016 _____ asteroids

3.017 _____ comets

3.018 _____ meteors

3.019 _____ meteorites

3.020 _____ sidereal day

3.021 _____ umbra

a. of spring

b. dark center of a shadow

c. rotation of earth relative to distant stars

d. 595 million miles

e. bright objects with nucleus, coma, and tail

f. does not have a moon

g. largest planet

h. thousands of "small planets" orbiting the sun

i. 11-year period

j. fall to earth

k. shooting stars

l. named after Jupiter

Complete these list (each answer, 2 points).

3.022   List the eight planets of the solar system in order of their distance from the sun:

a. _____   b. _____   c. _____

d. _____   e. _____   f. _____

g. _____   h. _____

Write the correct letter and answer on each line (each answer, 2 points).

3.023   The sun contains _____ percent of the mass of the solar system.
      a. 50   b. 80   c. 99

3.024   In the sun, hydrogen is converted to helium through _____ .
      a. heat convection   b. nuclear fusion   c. nuclear fission

3.025   The surface temperature of the sun is about _____°F.
      a. 10,000   b. 100,000   c. 59,000,000

3.026   The cooler temperature of sunspots is caused by a _____ .
      a. nuclear explosion   b. magnetic field   c. solar wind

3.027   The sun rotates on it axis once every _____ .
      a. 28 hours   b. 25 days 9 hours   c. 120 days

3.028   Spectacular eruptions of hot gases on the sun's surface are called _____ .
      a. solar earthquakes   b. prominences   c. solar volcanoes

3.029   Atomic particles from solar flares can cause _____ .
      a. Northern Lights   b. nuclear explosions   c. sunspots

3.030   Mercury has _____ moons.
      a. no   b. two   c. three

3.031   Long-period comets take _____ to orbit the sun.
      a. about 5 years   b. 200 or more years   c. much energy

3.032   About _____ meteorites reach the earth each year.
      a. 25   b. 100   c. 500

Answer these questions (each answer, 5 points).

3.033   What are some of the main characteristics of comets?

_____

_____

_____

_____

_____

_____

_____

_____

3.034   What is the difference between meteors, meteoroids, and meteorites?

_____

_____

_____

_____

_____

_____

_____

_____

_____

_____

78 / 98   SCORE _____   TEACHER _____ _____

initials   date

Before taking the LIFEPAC Test, you may want to do one or more of these self checks.

1. _____ Read the objectives. See if you can do them.
2. _____ Restudy the material related to any objectives that you cannot do.
3. _____ Use the **SQ3R** study procedure to review the material.
4. _____ Review all activities, Self Tests, and LIFEPAC vocabulary words.
5. _____ Restudy areas of weakness indicated by the last Self Test.